Longman Practice Exam Papers

GCSE Mathematics Intermediate

Brian Speed

Series editors:

Geoff Black and Stuart Wall

Titles available for GCSE

Biology

Chemistry

Mathematics (Intermediate)

Mathematics (Higher)

Physics

Science

Addison Wesley Longman Ltd,
Edinburgh Gate, Harlow,
CM20 2JE, England
and Associated Companies throughout the World

First Published 1998
Second impression 1998

ISBN 0 582 35647 4

British Library Cataloguing-in-Publication Data
A catalogue record for this book is available from the British Library.

Set in Times 11/13pt

Printed in Great Britain by Henry Ling Ltd at The Dorset Press, Dorchester, Dorset.

Contents

Editors' Preface

Longman Practice Exam Papers are written by experienced GCSE examiners and teachers. They will provide you with an ideal opportunity to practise under exam-type conditions before your actual school or college mocks or before the GCSE examination itself. As well as becoming familiar with the vital skill of pacing yourself through a whole exam paper, you can check your answers against examiner solutions and mark-schemes to assess the level you have reached.

Longman Practice Exam Papers can be used alongside the *Longman GCSE Study Guides* and *Longman Exam Practice Kits* to provide a comprehensive range of home study support as you prepare to take your GCSE in each subject covered.

How to use this book

One of the best ways to revise Mathematics is to answer questions.

- This book has four practice examination papers, which are very similar in style to the type you can expect to get when you take your Intermediate Level Mathematics GCSE examination. You can practise for both your mock and your actual examination with these papers – they will help you to fully prepare yourself.

- The solutions to the questions are given at the end of the practice papers. These tell you how the question should have been answered, and show you how many marks you would get in the examination for the solution you have worked out.

- There are also extra examiners' tips to help you realise the importance of some other information we can give you, and to help you with your revision.

- At the end of the book there is a mark analysis. This tells you what your mark means in terms of grades and suggests what you should do next.

- You need to use this book as part of your revision process. Make sure you revise the topics you had most difficulty with before attempting the next paper. This should mean that you will improve your marks as you work through the book.

- Give yourself time to answer each paper in one go if possible (but do encourage a helpful parent to bring you a welcome coffee, etc., halfway through).

- Find somewhere comfortable, with good light, and preferably with fresh air.

- Before you sit the first paper, read through the following guidelines, which are just as true for the real-life papers as they are for these practice papers.

  - Make sure you have the right equipment ready; pencil, pen, rubber, ruler, protractor, calculator (with either new or spare battery).

  - Read each question carefully at least twice – it's a shame to answer the wrong question, as you will not get the marks you deserve.

  - Underline key words while reading the question, also key bits of information.

  - Remember that the examiners only ask you questions that are on your syllabus, so you will have seen all these types of question before.

  - Look at the number of lines left for the answer as well as the number of marks – these give hints as to how much work is to be done to find the answer and how much working needs to be shown.

  - Do show your methods of solution clearly – you will get marks for a correct method even if you have got the final answer wrong.

  - Always give units in your solution, being careful to show area units and volume units correctly. There are always some marks available on the exam papers for the correct units being used.

  - Always think about rounding off the final answer. If the answer should be an integer (whole number), then make it so; if not, then try to round off to the same number of significant figures as the numbers shown in the question.

  - Work through the paper, keeping an eye on the clock – you do not want to be rushing your answers at the end of the two hours.

  - Attempt every question. If you make a guess, you cannot lose marks, whereas you could be lucky and find the right answer.

- Don't stop, use the full time, and go back and check. Check that you've read the question properly; you've put in your units; you've rounded off correctly – I know it can be tiresome, but it's worth it if you gain those extra marks that give you the grade you are seeking instead of just missing it!

- If you do sense that you are running out of time, just remember to do the things you can do well first.

- Don't forget, if you have done your revision justice already, have confidence – there will be nothing new in the questions, you'll be able to answer them all.

Longman Examination Board

General Certificate of Secondary Education

Mathematics – Intermediate Level

Paper 1

Time: 2 hours

Instructions

- Attempt as many questions as you can. Show all your working in the space provided.

- Make sure that your answer is clear, and state the units.

- If your calculator does not have a π button, take the value of π to be 3.142 unless otherwise instructed in the question.

Information for candidates

- The number of marks is given in brackets at the end of each question or part-question.

- Marks will not be deducted for wrong answers.

- This paper has 24 questions. The maximum mark for this paper is 100.

Number	Mark
1.	
2.	
3.	
4.	
5.	
6.	
7.	
8.	
9.	
10.	
11.	
12.	
13.	
14.	
15.	
16.	
17.	
18.	
19.	
20.	
21.	
22.	
23.	
24.	

Formula sheet

Area of triangle = $\frac{1}{2}$ × base × height

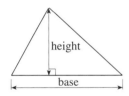

Pythagoras' Theorem = $a^2 + b^2 = c^2$

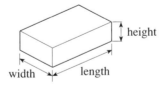

Trigonometry

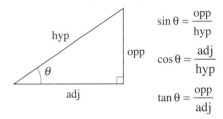

$$\sin \theta = \frac{\text{opp}}{\text{hyp}}$$

$$\cos \theta = \frac{\text{adj}}{\text{hyp}}$$

$$\tan \theta = \frac{\text{opp}}{\text{adj}}$$

Area of parallelogram = base × height

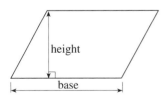

Volume of cuboid = length × width × height

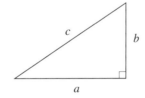

Volume of cylinder = $\pi r^2 h$
Curved surface of cylinder = $2\pi rh$

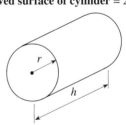

Area of trapezium = $\frac{1}{2}$ $(a + b)h$

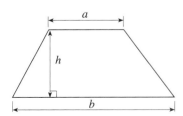

Circumference of circle = π × diameter
= 2 × π × radius
Area of circle = π × (radius)^2

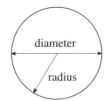

Volume of prism = area of cross section × length

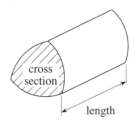

3

1. Calculate 8% of £240.

$$\frac{8}{240} \times 100 =$$

....

....

....

(2 marks)

2. Kevin is making a lawn in his back garden, and wants the area to be 40 m^2.

He wants the length to be 2 metres greater than the width.

His wife suggests making it 5 metres by 7 metres.

(a) Calculate the area of the lawn suggested by Kevin's wife.

.... $5 \times 7 = 35$ ....

....

(2 marks)

(b) Use a trial and improvement method to find the length and width of the lawn that will give an area of 40 m^2.

Give the dimensions correct to 1 decimal place.

Remember that the length must be 2 metres greater than the width.

....

....

....

....

....

....

(3 marks)

3. Which has the smaller value, $\frac{5}{8}$ or 0.63?

Explain how you reached your answer.

....

....

....

(2 marks)

4. The rule for a sequence is

Multiply the previous number by 2, then add 3.

The first three numbers in the sequence are:

$$3, 9, 21 \ldots$$

Work out the next three numbers in the sequence.

....

....

....

(3 marks)

5. Solve the equations below.

(a) $3 + 4x = 13$

....

....

(2 marks)

(b) $7x - 3 = 2x + 9$

....

....

....

(3 marks)

6. Describe an experiment for finding the probability of a matchbox landing on its edge when it is dropped.

....

....

....

....

(3 marks)

7. Draw an accurate net of a square-based pyramid, where the base length is 2 cm and each sloping edge is 1.8 cm.

(4 marks)

Turn over

8. The diagram is a conversion graph between £s and French francs.

    Use the graph to change:

    (a) (i) £5 to French francs

    ....

    (1 mark)

    (ii) £1.70 to French francs

    ....

    (1 mark)

    (b) (i) 30 French francs to £s

    ....

    (1 mark)

    (ii) 20 French francs to £s

    ....

    (1 mark)

9. Both wheels of the bicycle that James rode had a diameter of 60 cm.

    (a) What is the circumference of one of the wheels?

    ....

    ....

    ....

    ....

    (2 marks)

    James rode on his bike from home to school, a distance of about 1.5 km.

    (b) Approximately how many complete turns did one wheel make while James was riding his bike to school?

    ....

    ....

    ....

    (3 marks)

10. $P = M^2 - \dfrac{100}{M}$

    Calculate the value of P when $M = -2.5$

    ....

    ....

    ....

    ....

    (3 marks)

11. The solid shape shown falls over on to the shaded face.

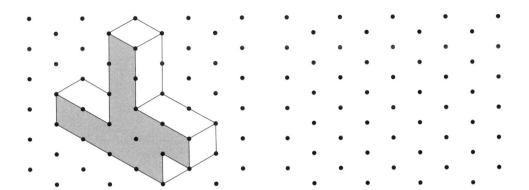

Draw on the isometric paper the shape after it has fallen over.

(3 marks)

12. 100 grams of Weetabix contain 11.2 grams of protein.

48 Weetabix weigh 900 grams.

How much protein will 1 Weetabix contain?

....

....

....

....

(4 marks)

13. The diagram shows two quadrilaterals labelled S and T.

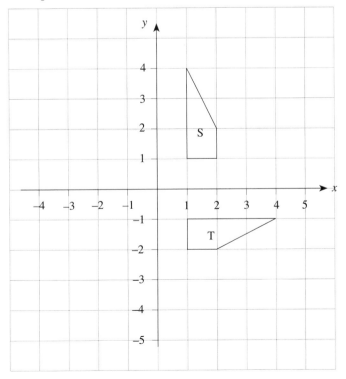

Turn over

(a) Describe the single transformation needed to move T to S.

....

....

....

(3 marks)

(b) Show on the diagram the reflection of S in the line $x = -1$.

....

....

....

(2 marks)

(c) Enlarge T from (4,0) with a scale factor of 2.

....

....

....

(2 marks)

14. Two bags contain coloured beads.

Bag A contains 4 blue beads and 1 white bead.

Bag B contains 2 blue beads and 3 white beads.

One bead is drawn at random from each bag.

(a) Complete the tree diagram and fill in the table to show the possible events.

(3 marks)

(b) What is the probability of getting 2 beads of the same colour?

....

....

....

....

(3 marks)

15. Bert is putting cats eyes in the middle of the road.

He is told to put them in a stretch of road 8 kilometres long.

(a) About how many miles are equivalent to 8 kilometres?

....

(1 mark)

(b) Bert knows that he needs one cats eye for every 20 yards of road.

(1760 yards = 1 mile)

How many cats eyes will Bert need for this job?

....

....

(2 marks)

(c) Use some of the data in this question to help you show that 1 metre is longer than 1 yard.

....

....

(2 marks)

16. The line $2y + 3x = 18$ is drawn on the grid below.

(a) On the grid, draw the line $y = 3x - 1$.

(3 marks)

(b) Use your graph to solve the simultaneous equations

$$2y + 3x = 18$$

$$y = 3x - 1$$

....

....

....

....

(2 marks)

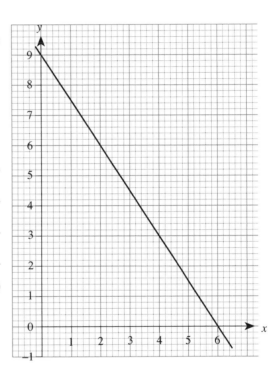

17. Sixty people were weighed in a nursing home.

The weight, w kg, of each person was recorded.

The data is shown in the table.

Weight, w kg	**Number of people**
$30 < w \le 40$	18
$40 < w \le 50$	27
$50 < w \le 60$	15

Turn over

Calculate an estimate of the mean weight of the people.

....

....

....

....

....

(5 marks)

18. Barry uses his calculator to work out

$$\frac{15.9 \times 4.3}{0.9 \times 7.5}$$

Show how you would estimate the answer to this calculation.

....

....

....

....

(3 marks)

19. The cost, £C, of a conference of n people at Bingham Park Manor is given by the formula $C = 15n + 70$

   (a) What is the cost of a conference with 40 people?

....

....

....

(2 marks)

   (b) (i) Rearrange this formula to make n the subject.

....

....

....

(2 marks)

Leave margin blank

(ii) The cost of a Green Party conference was £1225.

How many people were at that conference?

....

....

....

(2 marks)

20. Factorise fully $2x + 8x^2$

....

....

....

(2 marks)

21. Solve the inequality $t^2 < 25$

....

....

....

....

....

(2 marks)

22.

(a) Calculate AC.

....

....

....

....

(2 marks)

(b) Calculate BC.

....

....

....

....

(2 marks)

Turn over

(c) Calculate

    (i) angle x

....

....

....

(2 marks)

    (ii) angle y

....

....

....

(2 marks)

(d) Hence calculate AP.

....

....

....

(2 marks)

23. The diagrams show axes with the lines $y = x + 2$ and $x + y = 5$, both drawn and labelled.

Diagram 1   Diagram 2   Diagram 3

(a) On diagram 1 shade the region $y < x + 2$

(b) On diagram 2 shade the region $x + y > 5$

(c) On diagram 3 shade the region $y > 3$

(3 marks)

24. This statement was heard on TV the other night:

The only people who do not shop on a Sunday are Christians over 50.

Design a questionnaire you could use to see if the statement is true.

....

....

....

....

....

....

....

....

....

....

....

....

(3 marks)

Total: 100 marks

Longman Examination Board

General Certificate of Secondary Education

Mathematics – Intermediate Level

Paper 2

Time: 2 hours

Instructions

■ Attempt as many questions as you can.

■ Show all your working in the space provided.

■ Make sure that your answer is clear, and state the units.

■ If your calculator does not have a π button, take the value of π to be 3.142 unless otherwise instructed in the question.

Information for candidates

■ The number of marks is given in brackets at the end of each question or part-question.

■ Marks will not be deducted for wrong answers.

■ The maximum mark for this paper is 100.

■ A formulae sheet is printed on page 3.

Number	Mark
1.	
2.	
3.	
4.	
5.	
6.	
7.	
8.	
9.	
10.	
11.	
12.	
13.	
14.	
15.	
16.	
17.	
18.	

1.

Sea View Watersports Club			
Membership per year	£71		
Activity fees:	Water-skiing	Windsurfing	Sailing
Members per hour	£6.50	£2.75	£3.50
Non-members per hour	£11	£5.50	£7.75

Alison enjoys windsurfing, so she becomes a member of the Sea View Watersports Club for a year.

(a) One weekend she windsurfs from 3 p.m. to 5 p.m. on Saturday, and from 9 a.m. to midday on Sunday.

How much does this cost her?

....

....

(2 marks)

Leave margin blank

(b) She spends £373.50 altogether on membership and windsurfing for the year. How many hours has she spent windsurfing?

....

....

....

(3 marks)

2. A company employs 20 people.

   The manager plans to hold a works outing for them all.

   She wants to know which day of the week the majority of the employees would prefer for the outing.

   Design a suitable observation sheet to collect this information.

   Fill in your observation sheet as if you had carried out this survey.

   ....

   ....

   ....

   ....

   ....

   ....

   ....

   ....

   ....

   (3 marks)

3. The bar chart shows the results of a survey to find the number of children in a random sample of families.

Turn over

(a) How many families were included in this survey?

....

....

(2 marks)

(b) The results of this survey are to be shown on a pie chart.

Calculate the angle of the sector representing the number of families with 2 children.

....

....

....

....

(2 marks)

(c) Calculate the mean number of children per family.

....

....

....

....

....

....

(3 marks)

4.

In the diagram, triangle ABC is isosceles with BC = AC.

The lines AB and DC are parallel.

(a) Calculate angle CBA.

....

....

(2 marks)

(b) Calculate angle ACD.

....

....

(1 mark)

(c) If angle DAC is 80°, what can you say about:

(i) lines BC and AD?

....

(2 marks)

(ii) angles ABC and CDA?

....

(1 mark)

5. Geoffrey was playing cricket really well one weekend.

On Friday he scored x runs.

On Saturday he scored twice as many runs as he had scored on Friday.

On Sunday he scored 45 more runs than he had on Friday.

(a) Write down, in terms of x, the number of runs he scored

(i) on Saturday

....

(1 mark)

(ii) on Sunday

....

(1 mark)

(b) Altogether in these three days he scored 185 runs.

(i) Use this information to write down an equation in x.

....

....

(1 mark)

(ii) Solve your equation to find the number of runs Geoffrey scored on Friday.

....

....

....

(4 marks)

6. (a) Approximately one eighth of all British exports are sent to the USA.

(i) What fraction of British exports are sent to the rest of the world?

....

....

(1 mark)

(ii) In 1990 the value of exports to the USA was £13 000 million.

Calculate the estimated exports to the rest of the world.

....

....

....

(2 marks)

Turn over

(b) In 1995 Taylors Trousers exported clothes to the value of £450 000.

They set a target for 1996 to increase this by 8%.

(i) How much did they hope to export?

....

....

....

....

(2 marks)

(ii) In fact they exported clothes to the value of £490 000.

What percentage increase had they made?

....

....

....

....

(3 marks)

7. (a) The first four terms of a sequence are

3, 7, 11, 15, ...

Write down

(i) the seventh term of this sequence

....

....

(2 marks)

(ii) the nth term of this sequence

....

....

(2 marks)

(b) The nth term of another sequence is given by $3n + 8$

What is the least value of n which will give a term greater than 1000?

....

....

....

....

....

(3 marks)

Leave margin blank

8. A cylindrical can of Fizzo had a radius of 3.25 cm and a height of 11.5 cm.

   When the can was opened it was found to be only $\frac{7}{8}$ full.

   Calculate the volume, in millilitres, of drink in the can.

   ....

   ....

   ....

   ....

   ....

   ....

   (4 marks)

9. An English teacher did a survey on his students to find out how long they spent each week reading.
   He also gave the same students a spelling test.

   The results are as follows.

Spellings correct	7	7	9	10	10	11	12	13	12	13	13
Reading time, minutes	50	200	50	110	80	100	120	40	120	150	170

Spellings correct	15	15	16	16	17	18	18	19	19	20	20
Reading time, minutes	90	110	150	180	170	200	220	230	260	240	260

   (a) Draw a scatter diagram to illustrate these results.

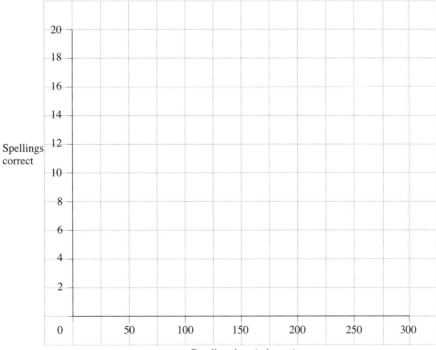

   (2 marks)

   Turn over

(b) Draw a line of best fit.

(1 mark)

(c) (i) Sheena took the spelling test the next day, after being absent. She got 14 spellings right. How many minutes each week would you expect her to read?

....

(1 mark)

(ii) Martin, who only reads for one hour each week, missed the spelling test. How many would you expect him to get right if he did take the test?

....

(1 mark)

10. (a) Jo put his 6 metre ladder up against a wall so that the foot of the ladder was 1 metre away from the wall.

How high up the wall did the ladder reach?

Give your answer to an appropriate degree of accuracy.

....

....

....

(3 marks)

6 m

1 m

(b) Joy has an adjustable ladder.

She wants to reach a window 5 metres up the wall, and to have the foot of the ladder 1 metre away from the wall.

How long should she make her ladder?

Give your answer to an appropriate degree of accuracy.

....

....

....

(3 marks)

11. Solve these simultaneous equations.

$$4m + 2t = 17$$
$$5m - 4t = 5$$

....

....

....

....

....

(5 marks)

12.

(a) Calculate the length DC, labelled x.

....

....

....

(2 marks)

(b) Calculate the size of angle y.

....

....

....

(2 marks)

(c) Use trigonometry to calculate the length BD.

....

....

....

(3 marks)

13. A new TV mast is to be built to serve three towns, Ayton, Brontin and Chidle.

The diagram below shows a scale plan representing the centres of the three towns.
The scale is 1 cm to 10 km.

(a) The mast is to be built so that it is exactly the same distance from both Ayton and Brontin.

● Brontin

● Ayton

● Chidle

Draw a line representing all the possible places satisfying this criterion.

(2 marks)

(b) The mast must be between 20 and 30 km from Chidle.

Show on your diagram the possible locations of the mast.

(3 marks)

Turn over

14. Keith and David are to play two games of chess.

They take it in turn to go first.

(a) When Keith goes first, the probability that he wins is $\frac{5}{8}$.

What is the probability that when Keith goes first, he does not win?

....

....

(1 mark)

(b) When David goes first, the probability that he wins is $\frac{1}{2}$.

The probability that the game is a draw is $\frac{1}{3}$.

Calculate the probability that when David goes first, he will not lose the game.

....

....

....

(2 marks)

(c) Calculate the probability that Keith wins both games.

....

....

(2 marks)

15. The duty free goods bought by each passenger on flight B105 were weighed.

The weights are summarised in the table below.

Weight of goods (Kg)	Frequency	Cumulative frequency
0 < weight ≤ 5	4	4
5 < weight ≤ 10	9	
10 < weight ≤ 15	17	
15 < weight ≤ 20	30	
20 < weight ≤ 25	22	
25 < weight ≤ 30	8	

(a) (i) Complete the cumulative frequency column.

(1 mark)

Leave margin blank

(ii) Draw a cumulative frequency diagram.

(2 marks)

(b) Use your graph to obtain an estimate of

(i) the median weight of goods for each passenger.

....

(1 mark)

(ii) the interquartile range

....

....

(2 marks)

16. Decide whether each of the following expressions represents: a volume (V), an area (A), a length (L), or none of these (N).

(i) $a^2b + ab^2$ ....

(ii) $a(a + b)$ ....

(iii) $a^2 - b$ ....

(iv) $ab + b^2$ ....

(note that a and b are lengths)

(4 marks)

17. $m = 3.7 \times 10^8$ and $p = 8.2 \times 10^{-5}$

Calculate the value of each of the following, giving your answers in standard form.

(a) mp

....

....

(2 marks)

(b) $m \div p$

....

....

(2 marks)

(c) $m + 5\,000\,000p$

....

....

....

(2 marks)

Turn over

18. (a) Complete the table of values for the equation

$$y = 5 \div x$$

x	1	2	2.5	4	5
$y = 5 \div x$	5				1

(1 mark)

(b) Draw a graph of $y = 5 \div x$.

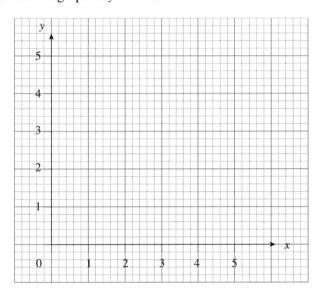

(2 marks)

(c) Use your graph to estimate a solution to the equation $\dfrac{5}{x} = 1.7$

....

....

(1 mark)

Total: 100 marks

Longman
Examination Board

General Certificate of Secondary Education

Mathematics – Intermediate Level

Paper 3

Time: 2 hours

Instructions

- Attempt as many questions as you can.

- Show all your working in the space provided.

- Make sure that your answer is clear, and state the units.

- If your calculator does not have a π button, take the value of π to be 3.142 unless otherwise instructed in the question.

Information for candidates

- The number of marks is given in brackets at the end of each question or part-question.

- Marks will not be deducted for wrong answers.

- The maximum mark for this paper is 100.

- A formula sheet is printed on page 3.

Number	Mark
1.	
2.	
3.	
4.	
5.	
6.	
7.	
8.	
9.	
10.	
11.	
12.	
13.	
14.	
15.	
16.	
17.	
18.	

1. Two typists advertise their costs as shown below.

Leave margin blank

Wendyword	**Quicktype**
Fixed charge £3	Fixed charge £8
plus 90p per page	plus 60p per page

(a) A formula for the total cost, £C, of n pages of typing by Wendyword is

$$C = 3 + 0.9n$$

Calculate the cost of having a 50-page booklet typed by Wendyword.

....

....

....

(2 marks)

Turn over

(b) (i) What will be the total cost of having a 50-page booklet typed by Quicktype?

....

....

(2 marks)

(ii) Write down a formula for calculating the total cost, £C, of n pages of typing by Quicktype.

....

....

(1 mark)

2. Margaret won £3700 on a lottery.

She decided to keep $\frac{2}{5}$ of this for herself. Margaret divided the rest between her husband, her daughter and a local charity in the ratio of 3 : 2 : 1.

(a) How much was left after Margaret kept her share?

....

....

....

(2 marks)

(b) How much did her daughter get?

....

....

....

(2 marks)

(c) What percentage of the win did her husband receive?

....

....

....

....

....

....

(3 marks)

3.

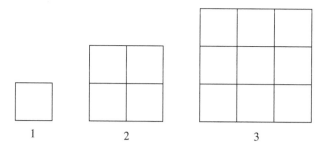

1   2   3

This is a sequence of square patterns.

The total number of squares in each pattern is shown in the table below.

Diagram	Number of squares
1	1
2	1 + 4 = 5
3	1 + 4 + 9 = 14

(a)   (i)   Draw the next two patterns in the sequence.

(1 mark)

(ii) Write down how many squares there are in each of your patterns.

....

....

....

....

(3 marks)

(b) Describe a method to work out the number of squares in the 10th pattern, **without drawing it.**

....

....

....

(1 mark)

4. I know from bitter experience that my bus to work is never early, and that the probability of it being on time is about 0.3

(a) What is the probability of my bus being late?

....

....

(1 mark)

Turn over

(b) What is the probability of my bus being on time for two days in a row?

....

....

(2 marks)

(c) I use the bus to go to work on about 250 days in the year.

On how many of these days can I expect the bus to be on time?

....

....

(2 marks)

5. (a) Sketch two different possible nets of a cube.

(2 marks)

(b) The diagram below is a tetrahedron. All the faces are equilateral triangles.

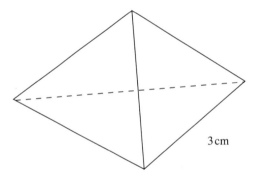

3 cm

Draw an accurate net of this tetrahedron.

(4 marks)

6. (a) How many sides has a nonagon?

....

(1 mark)

(b) Calculate the exterior angle of a regular nonagon.

....

....

(2 marks)

(c) Calculate the interior angle of a regular nonagon.

....

....

(2 marks)

(d) Why won't a regular nonagon tessellate?

....

....

....

(1 mark)

7. Jenny has to find, correct to two decimal places, the solution to the equation

$x^3 + x = 1$

(a) After about five minutes with her calculator she says, 'I know the answer is
between 0.6 and 0.7'

Show that Jenny is right.

....

....

....

....

(1 mark)

(b) Showing your working clearly, solve the equation $x^3 + x = 1$ to 2 decimal places.

....

....

....

....

....

....

(4 marks)

Turn over

8. Solve the following equations.

   (a) $4x - 3 = 11$

   ....

   ....

   ....

   (2 marks)

   (b) $20 + 3y = 8 - y$

   ....

   ....

   ....

   (3 marks)

9. The diagram shows two points, A (2,2) and B (4,3)

   (a) What is the gradient of the line AB?

   ....

   ....

   ....

   ....

   (2 marks)

   (b) If the line AB was extended, where would it cut through the y-axis?

   ....

   (1 mark)

   (c) Write down the equation of the straight line that the points A and B are on.

   ....

   ....

   (2 marks)

   (d) How long is the line AB?

   ....

   ....

   ....

   (3 marks)

10. The top diagram represents a grain hopper, in the shape of a prism, with the regular cross section as shown.

    (a) (i) Find the area of the regular cross section.

    ....

    ....

    ....

    (2 marks)

    (ii) Find the volume of the hopper.

    ....

    ....

    ....

    (3 marks)

    (b) Farmer Knowitt designed his own hopper with the dimensions as shown in the bottom diagram.

    (i) Find in terms of x the area of the regular cross section.

    ....

    ....

    (2 marks)

    (ii) The hopper should hold 25 m^3 of grain.

    Show that $6x^3 + 3x^2 = 25$

    ....

    ....

    ....

    (2 marks)

11. Wesley cycles from school to his grandfather's house 18 km away.

    He leaves school at 4 p.m. and cycles at a steady speed of 10 km/h for 45 minutes.

    Then he stops to talk to friends for half an hour.

    When he sets off again, Wesley cycles steadily and reaches the house at 6 p.m.

Turn over

(a) Draw a distance/time graph to illustrate Wesley's journey.

(3 marks)

(b) What was Wesley's speed, in km/h, for the last part of his journey?

....

....

(2 marks)

12. Hitan is doing a survey on healthy eating among 96 students in his year group.

Here are two questions from his survey:

1. How often do you eat chocolate?

2. Which is your favourite pudding from the following list?
(Underline your answer.)

yoghurt, sponge pudding, fruit, ice cream

(a) (i) Why is the first question a poor survey question?

....

....

(1 mark)

(ii) Write down a better version of question 1.

....

....

....

....

(1 mark)

(b) Here is a pie chart which represents the 96 replies to Hitan's second question.

Eight of the students said that fruit was their favourite pudding.

Complete the table below.

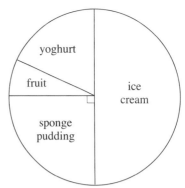

Type of pudding	Number of students choosing this type
yoghurt	
fruit	8
sponge pudding	
ice cream	
Total	96

(3 marks)

13. Albert has an ice cream van, and he notes the average daily temperature and how many ice creams he sells.

He made a scatter diagram for his results last year.

(a) What does the scatter diagram tell you?

....

....

....

(1 mark)

(b) There are 3 points on the graph that do not seem to fit into the correlation.

Choose one of those points and explain why it might be there.

....

....

....

(1 mark)

Number of ice creams sold

Temperature (°C)

(c) Albert hears the weather forecast for the next day. It says that the temperature will be about 15 °C all day.

About how many ice creams will he expect to sell on this day?

....

....

(1 mark)

Turn over

14. The formula $E = \frac{1}{2}mv^2$ gives energy in terms of mass and velocity.

(a) Rearrange the formula to make v the subject.

....

....

....

(2 marks)

(b) Calculate v when $E = 10^6$ and $m = 800$.

....

....

....

....

(2 marks)

15. I asked 50 married couples how long they had to wait for their partner to get ready when they were going out.

The results were as follows.

Time taken (t minutes)	Men	Women
$0 < t \leq 1$	1	0
$1 < t \leq 2$	2	1
$2 < t \leq 3$	6	2
$3 < t \leq 4$	19	7
$4 < t \leq 5$	11	15
$5 < t \leq 6$	7	18
$6 < t \leq 7$	3	5
$7 < t \leq 8$	1	2

(a) Draw a frequency polygon for each of the two distributions shown above.

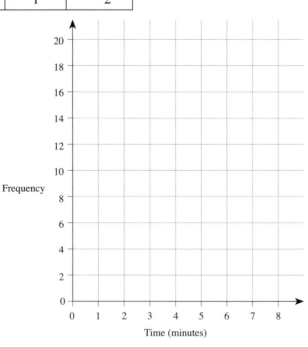

(3 marks)

(b) Comment on the difference between the two distributions.

....

....

(1 mark)

16. (a) Write down a triangle that is similar to ABE.

....

(1 mark)

(b) Calculate the following lengths:

(i) AB

....

....

....

(2 marks)

(ii) DE

....

....

....

(2 marks)

17. Solve these inequalities.

(a) $2x + 3 < 10$

....

....

(2 marks)

(b) $x^2 > 36$

....

....

....

(2 marks)

(c) $6x + 5 > 14x + 21$

....

....

....

(3 marks)

Turn over

18.

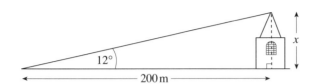

(a) From a point 200 metres from the foot of a church steeple, the angle of elevation of the top of the steeple is measured as 12°

Calculate the height (x) of the church steeple.

....

....

....

(3 marks)

(b) A kite was flying on a string 150 metres long. While flying, its angle of elevation was about 50°

Calculate the height (y) of the kite above the ground.

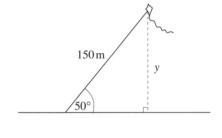

....

....

....

(3 marks)

Total: 100 marks

Longman Examination Board

General Certificate of Secondary Education

Mathematics – Intermediate Level

Paper 4

Time: 2 hours

Instructions

■ Attempt as many questions as you can.

■ Show all your working in the space provided.

■ Make sure that your answer is clear, and state the units.

■ If your calculator does not have a π button, take the value of π to be 3.142 unless otherwise instructed in the question.

Information for candidates

■ The number of marks is given in brackets at the end of each question or part-question.

■ Marks will not be deducted for wrong answers.

■ The maximum mark for this paper is 100.

■ A formula sheet is printed on page 3.

Number	Mark
1.	
2.	
3.	
4.	
5.	
6.	
7.	
8.	
9.	
10.	
11.	
12.	
13.	
14.	
15.	
16.	
17.	
18.	

---

1. For an away match, 984 supporters of Barnsley book to travel on the supporters club coach.

   Each coach can only hold 56 passengers.

   (a) How many coaches are needed to take all the supporters?

   ....

   ....

   ....

   (2 marks)

   (b) How many spare seats will there be?

   ....

   ....

   ....

   (2 marks)

Turn over

2. In the diagram, AB is parallel to DC.

    Calculate the sizes of the following angles.

    (a) x

    ....

    ....

    (1 mark)

    (b) y

    ....

    ....

    (1 mark)

    (c) w

    ....

    ....

    ....

    (2 marks)

3. Gwen saw a pack of pomegranates in the supermarket marked as 97p for 1 kg.

    She remembered last year seeing a similar pack marked at 87p for 2 lb.

    (a) Approximately how many pounds are equivalent to 1 kilogram ?

    ....

    (1 mark)

    (b) Has the price of pomegranates gone up or down from last year?
         Show all your working.

    ....

    ....

    ....

    ....

    (3 marks)

4. (a) The diameter of a circle is 1.2 metres.

(i) Calculate the circumference of this circle.

....

....

....

(2 marks)

(ii) Calculate the area of this circle.

....

....

....

(2 marks)

(b) The pillars in an ancient temple in Asia are cylindrical in shape.

The height of each pillar is equal to the circumference of its base.

The diameter of the base of one pillar is 1.2 metres.

Calculate its volume.

....

....

....

(2 marks)

5. A teacher did a survey to find out how his 24 pupils came to school one morning.

The results are shown in the pie chart.

(a) Calculate how many of these 24 pupils

(i) walked to school

....

....

....

....

(2 marks)

(ii) came to school by bus

....

....

....

(2 marks)

Turn over

(b) Imagine you are the teacher who is carrying out this survey.

Design the observation sheet that you would use to collect the required information.

Use your answers to part (a) to fill in your observation sheet.

....

....

....

....

....

....

....

....

....

....

....

(3 marks)

6. Look at the sequence 3, 5, 9, 17, 33

(a) Calculate the next term in the sequence.

....

....

(1 mark)

(b) Explain how you found the answer.

....

....

....

(2 marks)

7. (a) (i) Calculate the perimeter of the trapezium.

....

....

....

(1 mark)

5 cm

5 cm

4 cm

8 cm

15 cm

    (ii) Calculate the area of the trapezium.

....

....

....

(2 marks)

(b) C is a point 1 cm away from the perimeter of the trapezium on page 40.

     Draw a sketch to illustrate the locus of point C.

(4 marks)

8. Solve these simultaneous equations.

$$4x + y = 13$$

$$12x - y = 11$$

....

....

....

....

....

....

....

....

....

(4 marks)

9. Joseph and Kim are each given £1000 by their Grandma.

Fixed Term Bonds
£500 each
After 2 years can be cashed in to give
£635
(Cashed in early, redeemed
at face value
of £500 only)

Free Interest Account
6% interest
added to your balance
every 6 months

Turn over

(a) Joseph buys two Fixed Term Bonds.

What is the total amount he can cash them in for after two years?

....

....

(1 mark)

(b) Kim puts his £1000 into the Free Interest Account.

How much will he have in the account after

(i) 6 months

....

....

(2 marks)

(ii) 1 year

....

....

(2 marks)

(iii) 2 years

....

....

(2 marks)

10. The density of cedar wood is 0.57 g/cm^3.

What is the weight of a rectangular block of cedar wood with dimensions

4 cm by 5 cm by 12 cm?

....

....

....

....

....

(3 marks)

11. What is the smallest integer value of n that satisfies the inequality $5^n > 5000$?

....

....

....

....

....

(2 marks)

12.

(a) Draw one more triangle on the diagram so that the final picture is symmetrical about the dotted line. Label this triangle D.

(1 mark)

(b) What is the equation of the dotted line?

....

....

(1 mark)

(c) Describe fully the single transformation that will transform

(i) triangle B on to triangle C

....

....

....

(3 marks)

Turn over

(ii) triangle A on to triangle C

....

....

....

(2 marks)

13. (a) Solve $5(2x + 3) + 4(x - 2) = 14$

....

....

....

....

(3 marks)

(b) When Isaac Newton was x years old, he noticed that if he multiplied his age by 9 and subtracted it from 100 the answer was his age.

(i) Write down an equation in x from Isaac Newton's observation.

....

....

(1 mark)

(ii) How old was he when he noticed this?

....

....

(2 marks)

14. The 4 towns Alitown, Hope, Benton and Eden are all close to one another, as shown in the diagram.

Alitown is due North of Benton, and Eden is due East of both Hope and Benton.

(a) Calculate the distance from Hope to Alitown.

....

....

....

....

....

....

(3 marks)

Leave margin blank

(b) Calculate the bearing of Alitown from Eden.

....

....

....

(3 marks)

(c) Calculate the distance from Hope to Eden.

....

....

....

(3 marks)

15. On an island there are 100 churches, all with different numbers of members. The numbers of members in the churches are summarised in the table.

Members (m)	$0 < m \le 20$	$20 < m \le 40$	$40 < m \le 60$	$60 < m \le 80$	$80 < m \le 100$
Number of churches	8	29	38	17	8

(a) Calculate an estimate of the mean number of members per church.

....

....

....

....

(2 marks)

(b) Draw a cumulative frequency diagram.

(2 marks)

Turn over

(c) (i) Use your graph to estimate the median number of members per church.

....

(1 mark)

(ii) Calculate the interquartile range.

....

....

....

(3 marks)

(iii) Only the churches with over 65 members can have a minister of their own. How many of these churches can have a minister of their own?

....

....

(2 marks)

16. Here is a game for 2 players.

It is played with a bag containing 7 white balls and 4 black balls. All the balls are the same size and weight.

The players take it in turns to pick out one ball without looking. The first person to pick out two balls the same colour wins.

This is what happened on their first turns.

Player 1   Player 2

(a) Player 1 now picks another ball.

(i) What is the probability that player 1 will win on this turn?

....

....

(2 marks)

(ii) What is the probability that player 1 will not win on this turn?

....

....

(2 marks)

(b) (i) Write down the four different ways that player 1 could win the game after two goes.

....

....

....

....

....

(1 mark)

(ii) What is the probability that player 1 will win after two goes?

....

....

....

....

....

(3 marks)

17. (a) One grain of rice weighs 1.7×10^{-3} grams.

How many grains of rice will you get in 1 kilogram?

....

....

....

(2 marks)

(b) 1 kilogram of sand will contain approximately 20 000 000 000 grains of sand.

What is the weight of one grain of sand?

....

....

(2 marks)

Turn over

18. A container is filled with water at a steady rate.

The diagram below is the first part of a sketch graph showing the height of the water in the container compared with the time.

The diagram shows the water level has reached point A on the container, and line xy on the graph represents this height and the time taken to reach it.

Complete the sketch graph to the point where the container is full.

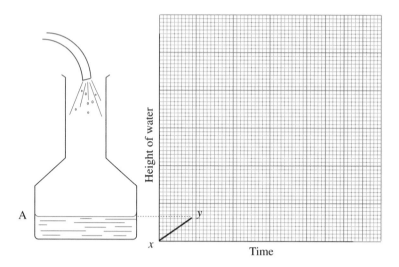

(5 marks)

Total: 100 marks

Solutions to practice exam papers

Please read this explanation of the marking system used for the practice exam papers, before you check your solutions.

The following abbreviations are shown next to each solution.

- **M1** – which means 1 mark has been given for a correct method.

- **A1** – which means 1 mark has been given for the correct answer.

- **B1** – which means 1 mark has been given for a particular part of the answer.

Examiners use M and A marks like this on many occasions when marking. This is because if they see the wrong answer, then they can still give you the method mark that goes with the question. Note also that examiners NEVER give a mark as **A1** without also giving the **M1** that goes with it.

Use the following solutions to mark your papers, then look at the mark analysis on page 72.

Solutions to Paper 1

1. $240 \times 8 \div 100 = £19.20$ **M1 A1   2 marks**

> **TIP**
> You score 1 mark for a correct method shown and 1 mark for the correct answer.

---

2. (a) $5 \times 7 = 35 \text{ m}^2$ **M1 A1   2 marks**

(b) Let the width be x, then $x \times (x + 2) = 40$.

Solve by trial and improvement, as shown here:

Trial (x)	Area	
5	$5 \times 7 = 35$	too small
6	$6 \times 8 = 48$	too big **M1**
5.5	$5.5 \times 7.5 = 41.25$	too big
5.4	$5.4 \times 7.4 = 39.96$	too small **M1**

x is between 5.4 and 5.5, so try 5.45 to see which is the nearest solution.

5.45	$5.45 \times 7.45 = 40.6025$	too big

This shows that 5.4 is the closest.

Therefore, the width is 5.4 m and the length is 7.4 m.   **A1   3 marks**

TIP

You score 1 mark for finding that the solution is between 5 and 6; you score another mark for showing that the solution is between 5.4 and 5.5. The final mark is given for the correct solution.

Note, you will usually only earn the final mark if you have shown WHY the solution is the nearest one, as shown above.

3. $\frac{5}{8} = 0.625$ **M1**

This is smaller than 0.63   **A1**   **2 marks**

TIP

You score 1 mark for showing $\frac{5}{8}$ is the same as 0.625, and the next mark for stating that it is smaller than 0.63

4. $\dot{4}5, 93, 189$ 1 mark given for each correct number   **3 marks**

TIP

If you get the first answer wrong, as long as you work out the next answer correctly from your wrong number, you will still gain 2 marks.

5. (a) $4x = 13 - 3 = 10$ **M1**

   $x = 10 \div 4 = 2.5$ **A1**   **2 marks**

   (b) $7x - 2x = 9 + 3$ **M1**

   $5x = 12$ **M1**

   $x = 2.4$ **A1**   **3 marks**

6. Either drop one matchbox a lot of times, or drop a lot of matchboxes a few times. Let the total number be N.   **M1**

Count how many times it falls on its edge, call this E.   **M1**

The probability is the fraction $\dfrac{E}{N}$ **A1**   **3 marks**

7. There are quite a few different ways of drawing this net accurately. One of these ways is shown below.

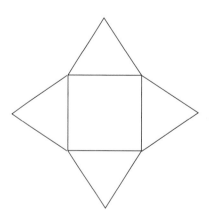

You score 1 mark for a correct looking net regardless of size.

You score 1 mark for the square being accurate at 2 cm by 2 cm and 1 mark for a triangle being drawn accurately with sloping edge 1.8 cm.

The final mark is given if all four triangles are drawn accurately.   **4 marks**

8. (a) (i) 43.5 francs (ii) 15 francs   1 mark each

(b) (i) £3.45   (ii) £2.30   1 mark each   **4 marks**

 TIP

The marks are given for accurate readings from the graph. A small deviation from the above readings (1 franc or 0.1 pound) is acceptable.

9. (a) $\pi \times 60 = 188$ cm   **M1 A1   2 marks**

You would be expected to round off here to either 2 or 3 significant figures.

(b) $1.5 \times 1000 \times 100 \div 188 = 797.8$ **M1 A1**

$$= 800 \quad \textbf{A1} \quad \textbf{3 marks}$$

10. $(-2.5)^2 - 100/-2.5 = P$ **M1 for the correct substitution**

6.25   +   40 $= 46.25$ **A1 + A1   3 marks**

 TIP

One mark is gained for simply substituting correctly as shown; the next mark is given for calculating both **6.25** and **40** correctly. The last mark is given if the final answer is correct.

11.

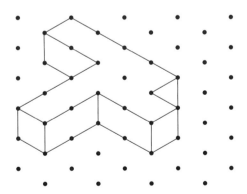

You score 3 marks if you have drawn the shape correctly; 2 marks if you have, at most, two lines incorrect; 1 mark if you have, at most, four lines incorrect.   **3 marks**

12. One Weetabix weighs $900 \div 48 = 18.75$ grams.   **M1 A1**

18.75 grams of Weetabix contain $^{11.2}/_{100} \times 18.75$ **M1**

$$= 2.1 \text{ grams of protein} \quad \textbf{A1} \quad \textbf{4 marks}$$

13. (a) A rotation of 90° anticlockwise around (0,0). **M1 A1 A1   3 marks**

You score 1 mark for stating that it is a rotation; 1 mark for 90° anticlockwise; and one mark for (0,0).

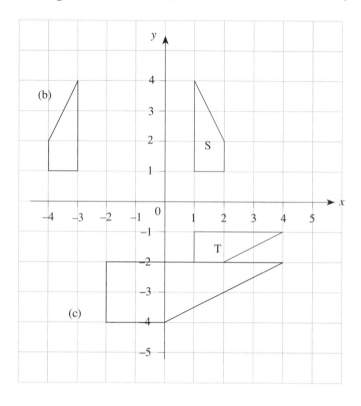

4 marks

For each transformation, you score 1 mark for moving the shape with the right TYPE of transformation, and the other mark for it being in the correct place.

TIP
Remember to fully explain the transformation – do not just name the type.

---

14. (a) you score **B1** for correctly placing ⅕; **B1** for the bag B column correct; **B1** for the final table of events correct.   **3 marks**

(b) B B or W W

$$\frac{4}{5} \times \frac{2}{5} + \frac{1}{5} \times \frac{3}{5} = \frac{8}{25} + \frac{3}{25} = \frac{11}{25}$$

You score **M1** for multiplying the correct fractions; **M1** for adding your answers together; and **A1** for getting to the correct answer of $\frac{11}{25}$.   **3 marks**

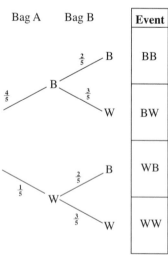

15. (a) 5   **B1**   **1 mark**

TIP
This is a fact you should know.

(b) $\dfrac{5 \times 1760}{20} = 440$ **M1 A1   2 marks**

(c) 8 km   = 8000 m

5 miles   = 8800 yards   **M1**

8000 m   = 8800 yards   **A1**

so 1 metre is longer   **2 marks**

16. (a) Choose three points that fit the equation $y = 3x - 1$ and plot them as shown.

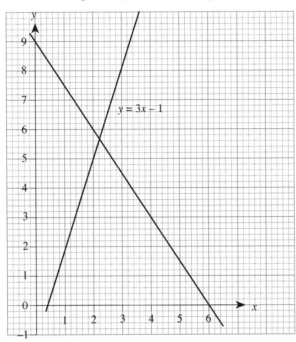

3 marks

You will score 3 marks if this line is drawn correctly. If it is not drawn correctly, you will score 1 mark provided you have plotted one point accurately.

TIP

To plot a straight line, always use three points.

(b) Your answer must be taken from your graph – the point where the two lines cross.

This should be close to $(2.2, 5.7)$. You will score 1 mark for each number, correct to 1 decimal place, taken from your intersection point.   **2 marks**

17. $\dfrac{(35 \times 18) + (45 \times 27) + (55 \times 15)}{(18 + 27 + 15)}$ **M1 M1**

M1

$= \dfrac{2670}{60} = 44.5 \text{ kg}$ **M1 A1   5 marks**

You will score 1 mark for using the middle of the class and multiplying that by the frequency. The next mark is for adding these products together.

You also score a mark for adding together all the frequencies.

The final 2 marks are given for dividing these totals and doing this correctly.

> **TIP**
>
> Make sure you do not make the common error of simply adding 18, 27 and 15, then dividing by 3.

18. $\dfrac{16 \times 4}{1 \times 8} = \dfrac{64}{8}$ or $\dfrac{16}{2} = 8$

You score **M1** for showing how you round off each figure to something suitable, then another **M1** for combining the numbers in such a way as to calculate the answer. You then score **A1** for the estimation of 8. **3 marks**

There are many other ways you could have rounded off these numbers, for example,

$\dfrac{16 \times 4.5}{8 \times 0.9} = 2 \times 5 = 10$

> **TIP**
>
> As long as you round off to make the calculation easy to do without a calculator, you will gain marks.

19. (a) C = $(40 \times 15) + 70 = £670$ **M1 A1   2 marks**

  (b) (i) $15n = C - 70$ **B1**

  $n = \dfrac{C - 70}{15}$ **B1**

  (ii) $\dfrac{1225 - 70}{15} = 77$ **M1 A1   4 marks**

20. $2x\,(1 + 4x)$ **B2   2 marks**

If you partly factorised it, as $2\,(x + 4x^2)$ or $x\,(2 + 8x)$, you score **B1.**

21. $t < 5$ and $t > -5$ **B1 + B1   2 marks**

> **TIP**
>
> Look out for the negative solution in this type of inequality; most people forget to include this in their solution.

22. (a) $AC^2 = 1^2 + 2^2$ **M1**

  $AC = \sqrt{5} = 2.236$ cm **A1   2 marks**

(b) $BC^2 = 3^2 - 5 = 4$ **M1**

    $BC = 2$ cm   **A1**   **2 marks**

(c) (i) $\tan x = 1/2$ **M1**

      $x = 26.6°$ **A1**   **2 marks**

  (ii) $\sin y = \frac{2}{3}$ **M1**

      $y = 41.8°$ **A1**   **2 marks**

(d) $AP = 3 \cos 68.4$ **M1**

    $= 1.1$ cm   **A1**   **2 marks**

TIP

You would usually score marks here even if you had more decimal places in your answers, as long as they were still correct.

23.

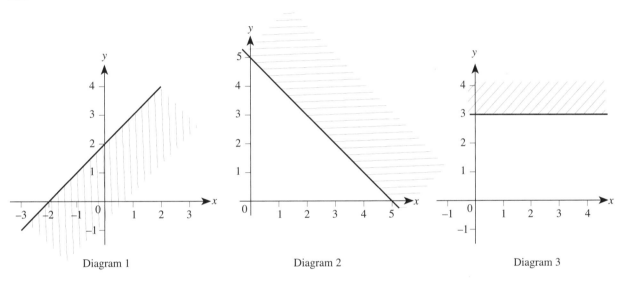

Diagram 1   Diagram 2   Diagram 3

You will score 1 mark for each correct diagram.   **3 marks**

24. You need three simple questions like:

Do you shop on a Sunday?   **B1**

Are you a Christian?   **B1**

Are you over 50?   **B1**   **3 marks**

TIP

Each question you use must be able to be answered simply, either with a yes or no, or with a full range of responses for each question.

Total: 100 marks

Solutions to Paper 2

1. (a) £2.75 × 5 = £13.75   **M1 A1   2 marks**

   (b) £373.50 − £71 = £302.50   **M1**

   £302.50 ÷ £2.75 = 110 hours   **M1 A1   3 marks**

2. You may ask the question 'Which day of the week would you prefer for the outing?'

Monday	111	
Tuesday	11	
Wednesday	̶L̶H̶1 1	
Thursday	11	
Friday	̶L̶H̶1	
Saturday	1	
Sunday	1	

You score **M1** for having all the days of the week on the observation sheet, **M1** for the space left to put responses in, and **A1** for the correct use of tallies in that space.   **3 marks**

> **TIP**
>
> Giving the question at the beginning would not be expected, but it is not wrong to include it.

3. (a) 10 + 25 + 36 + 19 + 5 = 95   **M1 A1   2 marks**

   (b) $\dfrac{36}{95} \times 360 = 136°$ **M1 A1   2 marks**

   (c) $(0 \times 10) + (1 \times 25) + (2 \times 36) + (3 \times 19) + (4 \times 5) = 174$ **M1**

   174 ÷ 95 = 1.8   **M1 A1   3 marks**

4. (a) (180 − 80) ÷ 2 = 50°   **M1 A1   2 marks**

   (b) 50°   **B1   1 mark**

   (c) (i) parallel and the same length   **B1 + B1   2 marks**

   (ii) they are the same (50°)   **B1   1 mark**

5. (a) (i) $2x$ (ii) $x + 45$ **B1 + B1   2 marks**

   (b) (i) $x + 2x + x + 45 = 185$ **B1   1 mark**

   (ii) $4x = 185 − 45 = 140$ **B1 + B1**

   $x = \dfrac{140}{4} = 35$ **M1 A1   4 marks**

6. (a) (i) $\frac{7}{8}$ **B1**   **1 mark**

   (ii) £13 000 × 7 =   **M1**

   = £91 000 million   **A1**   **2 marks**

TIP

The common error is to forget the million

(b) (i) $450\,000 \times \dfrac{8}{100} = 36\,000$ **M1**

   $36\,000 + 450\,000 = £486\,000$ **A1**   **2 marks**

   (or £450 000 × 1.08 = £486 000)

   (ii) $\dfrac{490\,000 - 450\,000}{450\,000} \times 100 = 8.9\%$

You score **M1** for setting up your fraction correctly, **M1** for multiplying your fraction by 100, and **A1** for the correct answer.   **3 marks**

7. (a) (i) 19, 23   **M1**

   so the seventh term is 27   **A1**   **2 marks**

   (ii) $4n - 1$

You score **B1** for the $4n$ and **B2** if you give the nth term in full.   **2 marks**

(b) $3n + 8 > 1000$ **M1**

   $3n \quad > 992$

   $n \quad > 330.6$ **A1**

so the smallest n will be 331   **A1**   **3 marks**

8. volume of can = $\pi \times 3.25^2 \times 11.5$ **M1**

   = 381.6 cm^3 **A1**

TIP

Any accuracy using more than 2 significant figures is acceptable here.

drink = $381.6 \times \dfrac{7}{8} = 333.9$ cm^3 **M1**

   = 334 millilitres   **A1**   **4 marks**

Your answer should be left at either 3 or 4 significant figures.

9.

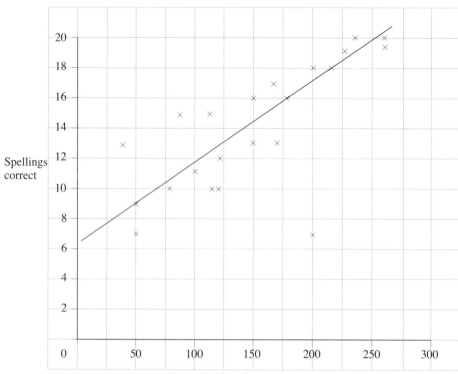

Reading time (minutes)

(a) You score 2 marks for the scatter diagram if all the points are plotted correctly. If you have made an error in plotting one or two points, you will only score 1 mark. **2 marks**

(b) There are many different correct places for the line of best fit, as long as you follow the trend and are close to the line shown in the diagram, you will score 1 mark. **1 mark**

(c) (i) The reading is from YOUR line of best fit, reading across from 14.

Your answer may well be close to 140 minutes. You score 1 mark. **1 mark**

　　(ii) This reading is also from YOUR line of best fit, reading up from 60 minutes. Your answer may well be close to 9 or 10. You score 1 mark. **1 mark**

10. (a) $H^2 = 6^2 - 1^2$ **M1**

$H = \sqrt{35} = 5.916$ **M1**

$= 5.9$ m **A1** **3 marks**

(b) $L^2 = 5^2 + 1^2$ **M1**

$L = \sqrt{26} = 5.099$ **M1**

$= 5.1$ m **A1** **3 marks**

TIP

Your answers need to have been sensibly rounded. In this context, that will be to either 2 or 3 significant figures.

11. $8m + 4t = 34$ **M1**

$\underline{5m - 4t = 5}$ **M1**

add $13m = 39$ **M1**

$m = 3$ **A1**

substitute

$24 + 4t = 34$ **M1**

$t = 2.5$ **A1** **5 marks**

TIP
You must show the correct method for solving simultaneous equations. if you do not get the answer right, this is the only way that you will gain any marks at all.

12. (a) $\dfrac{DC}{100} = \tan 40$ **M1**

$DC = 100 \tan 40 = 83.9$ m **A1** **2 marks**

(b) $\sin y = \dfrac{100}{300}$ **M1**

$y = 19.5°$ **A1** **2 marks**

(c) $\dfrac{100}{BD} = \cos 40$ **M1**

$BD = \dfrac{100}{\cos 40}$ **M1**

$= 130.5$ m **A1** **3 marks**

TIP
Because this is not a real-life situation, you would not lose marks if you did not round off your final answers. But I would recommend that you always think about rounding off answers like this as if they *were* real-life situations, then you will not get caught out unexpectedly.

13.

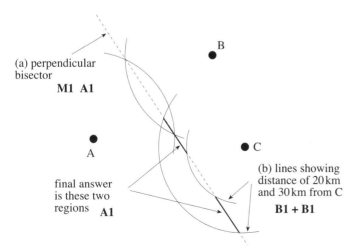

(a) perpendicular bisector
M1 A1

B

(b) lines showing distance of 20 km and 30 km from C
B1 + B1

A

C

final answer is these two regions **A1**

(a) **2 marks** (b) **3 marks**

14. (a) $1 - \frac{5}{8} = \frac{3}{8}$ **B1**   **1 mark**

(b) $(\frac{1}{2} + \frac{1}{3}) = \frac{5}{6}$ **M1 A1**   **2 marks**

(c) $\frac{5}{8} \times \frac{1}{6} = \frac{5}{48}$ **M1 A1**   **2 marks**

15. (a) (i) The cumulative frequencies are 4, 13, 30, 60, 82, 90 **B1**   **1 mark**

(ii)

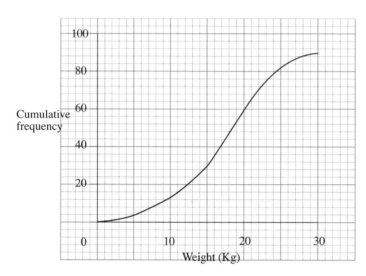

You score **B1** for correctly plotting the points, and you score 1 mark for drawing either a smooth curve through all the points, or the cumulative frequency polygon. **2 marks**

(b) The readings are from YOUR graph.

(i) the median is about 18.5 kg **B1 1 mark**

(ii) UQ – LQ = 21.5 – 13 = 8.5 **M1 A1**   **2 marks**

16. (i). V (ii) A (iii) N (iv) A 1 mark each **4 marks**

17. (a) 3.03×10^4 **2 marks**

(b) 4.5×10^{12} **2 marks**

(c) 3.7×10^8 or 3.7000041×10^8 **2 marks**

You score 1 mark for the first part of the standard form number, this can be any accuracy of 2 or more significant figures. You score another mark for the second part including the '$\times 10$'.

TIP

If you give the calculator display, e.g. 4.5 ^{12}, you will lose marks.

18. (a) The completed bottom row should look like this.

y	5	2.5	2	1.25	1

You score 1 mark if it is all correct. **1 mark**

(b)

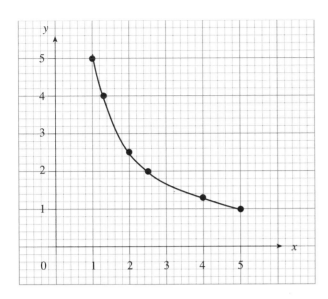

You score 1 mark for correctly plotting the points and 1 mark for a smooth curve. **2 marks**

(c) From YOUR graph, the answer should be about 2.9 **B1 1 mark**

> **TIP**
>
> Remember, you should always draw a graph and use it. Even if the graph is wrong, you can still get marks for taking readings from it.

Total: 100 marks

Solutions to Paper 3

1. (a) $C = 3 + (0.9 \times 50) = £48$ **M1 A1 2 marks**

   (b) (i) $8 + (0.6 \times 50) = £38$ **M1 A1 2 marks**

   (ii) $C = 8 + 0.6n$ **B1 1 mark**

2. (a) $3700 \times \frac{3}{5} = £2220$ **M1 A1 2 marks**

   (b) $2220 \times \frac{2}{6} = £740$ **M1 A1 2 marks**

   (c) $2220 \times \frac{3}{6} = £1110$ **B1**

   $$\frac{1110}{3700} \times 100 = 30\%$$ **M1 A1 3 marks**

3. (a) (i)

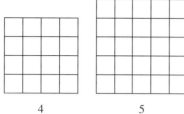

4   5

                                            B1   **1 mark**

    (ii) pattern 4 $1 + 4 + 9 + 16 = 30$ **M1**   **A1**

           pattern 5 $1 + 4 + 9 + 16 + 25 = 55$ **A1**   **3 marks**

    (b) add up the first ten square numbers (385)   **B1**   **1 mark**

4. (a) $1 - 0.3 = 0.7$ **B1**   **1 mark**

    (b) $0.3 \times 0.3 = 0.09$ **M1 A1**   **2 marks**

    (c) $250 \times 0.3 = 75$ **M1 A1**   **2 marks**

5. (a) There are several possible correct nets, the most obvious are probably those shown here.

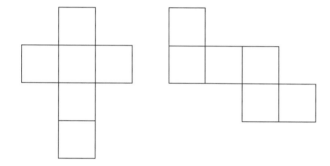

        You score 1 mark for each correct diagram.   **2 marks**

    (b) There are several different ways to draw the shape, the simplest is perhaps this one.

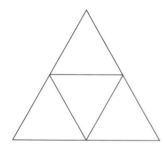

        You score four marks if the shape is all correct.   **4 marks**

        If it is not all correct, you earn marks as follows:

        M1 for a correct looking net (doesn't have to be accurate)

        B1 for the first correct sized triangle,

        B1 for the second accurate triangle.

TIP

The accuracy looked for in almost all cases is to be no more than 1 millimetre out and to be no more than 1° out.

6. (a) 9 **B1** **1 mark**

   (b) $360 \div$ your $9 = 40°$ **M1 A1** **2 marks**

   (c) $180 -$ your $40 = 140°$ **M1 A1** **2 marks**

   (d) because the interior angle is not a factor of $360°$ **B1** **1 mark**

7. (a) $(0.6)^3 + 0.6 = 0.816$ too low

   $(0.7)^3 + 0.7 = 1.043$ too high

   You need to show both the above to earn the one mark. **1 mark**

   (b) 0.68 **4 marks**

   You should have shown clear trials of two decimal place numbers between 0.6 and 0.7; this earns you your first mark.

   You should find the solution is between 0.68 and 0.69; this earns you 1 mark. You earn another mark for trying 0.685 in order to find which is the nearer of the 2 decimal place numbers you have. The last mark is for the correct solution of 0.68

> **TIP**
> You MUST show the complete method here to be sure of gaining ALL the marks.

8. (a) $4x = 14$ **M1**

   $x = 3.5$ **A1** **2 marks**

   (b) $3y + y = 8 - 20$ **M1**

   $4y = -12$ **M1**

   $y = -3$ **A1** **3 marks**

9. (a) vertical distance divided by horizontal distance **M1**

   this gives $\frac{1}{2}$ **A1** **2 marks**

   (b) $y = 1$ **B1** **1 mark**

   (c) $y = \frac{1}{2}x + 1$

   You score two marks if the full equation is correct, and 1 mark if only the $\frac{1}{2}x$ is correct. **2 marks**

   (d) $L^2 = 1^2 + 2^2$ **M1**

   $L = \sqrt{5} = 2.24$ **M1 A1** **3 marks**

> **TIP**
> You will get your accuracy marks here for any rounding of the correct answer with 2 or more significant figures.

10. (a) (i) $(2 \times 1.5) + \frac{1}{2}(1.5 \times 0.5) = 3.375 \text{ m}^2$ **M1 A1** **2 marks**

    (ii) your $3.375 \times 5 = 16.875 \text{ m}^3$ **M1 A1**

    (both units correct will earn you another **B1**) **3 marks**

(b) (i) $2x^2 + x$ **B1 + B1**   **2 marks**

(ii) $3x(2x^2 + x) = 25$ **M1**

$6x^3 + 3x^2 = 25$ **M1**   **2 marks**

11. (a)

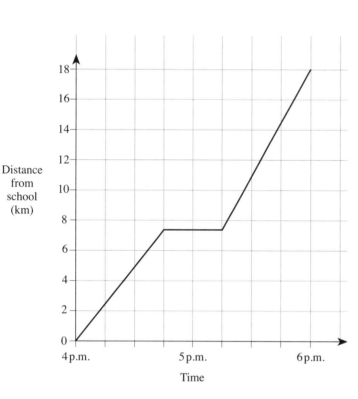

3 marks

You score **M1** for the first line being at the correct gradient, **M1** for the stop of 30 minutes being drawn correctly, and **M1** for completing the graph to (6 p.m., 18).

(b) 10.5 kilometres in 45 minutes   **M1**

Any answer between 14 km/h (± 0.5)   **A1**   **2 marks**

12. (a) (i) Too vague, you need to give all the possible ranges for the answers.   **B1**   **1 mark**

(ii) How often do you eat chocolate?

every day   ☐   at least once a week   ☐

at least once a month   ☐   never   ☐   **B1**   **1 mark**

(b) ice cream = $\frac{1}{2} \times 96 = 48$ **B1**

sponge pudding = $\frac{1}{4} \times 96 = 24$ **B1**

yoghurt = $96 - (48 + 24 + 8) = 16$ **B1**   **3 marks**

13. (a) The warmer the weather, the more ice creams he sells. **B1** **1 mark**

(b) There are many different possible answers; you could have said something like 'a cold bank holiday', or 'it was cold, but a fête was happening'. **B1** **1 mark**

(c) 150 **B1** **1 mark**

14. (a) $v^2 = \dfrac{2E}{m}$ **M1**

$v = \sqrt{\left(\dfrac{2E}{m}\right)}$ **A1** **2 marks**

(b) $\sqrt{\left(\dfrac{2 \times 10^6}{800}\right)} = 50$ **M1 A1** **2 marks**

15. (a)

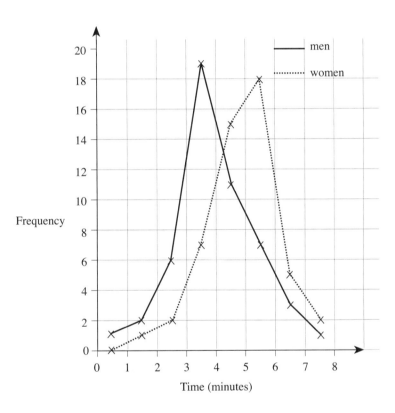

3 marks

You score **M1** for showing you know what a frequency polygon is; **M1** for plotting at the mid-point intervals; **A1** for plotting both distributions correctly.

(b) The women had to wait longer than the men. **B1** **1 mark**

TIP

Don't concentrate on the shape of the graph; put the interpretation into exactly what it means in the real-life situation.

16. (a) ACD **B1** **1 mark**

(b) (i) $\dfrac{AB}{12} = \dfrac{5}{8}$ **M1**

   $AB = 7.5$ cm   **A1**   **2 marks**

(ii) $\dfrac{AD}{7} = \dfrac{8}{5} \Rightarrow AD = 11.2$ **M1**

   $DE = 4.2$ **A1 2 marks**

17. (a) $2x < 7$ **M1**

   $x < 3.5$ **A1**   **2 marks**

(b) $x > 6$ and $x < -6$ **B1 + B1**   **2 marks**

TIP
Do not forget the negative solution.

(c) $5 - 21 > 14x - 6x$ **M1**

   $-16 > 8x$ **M1**

   $-2 > x$ or $x < -2$ **A1**   **3 marks**

18. (a) $\dfrac{x}{200} = \tan 12$ **M1**

   $x = 200 \tan 12 = 42.5$ m   **M1 A1**   **3 marks**

(b) $\dfrac{y}{150} = \sin 50$ **M1**

   $y = 150 \sin 50 = 115$ m   **M1 A1**   **3 marks**

TIP
It's worth remembering that trigonometry questions will ALWAYS appear on your paper and are worth between 4 and 9 marks.

Total: 100 marks

Solutions to Paper 4

1. (a) $984 \div 56 = 17.57$ **M1**

   so 18 coaches are needed   **A1**   **2 marks**

(b) $(18 \times 56) - 984 = 24$ **M1 A1 2 marks**

2. (a) 20° **B1** **1 mark**

(b) $180 - 65 = 115°$ **B1** **1 mark**

(c) $115 - 30 = 85°$ **M1 A1** **2 marks**

3. (a) 2.2 **B1** **1 mark**

(b) last year's price was $\dfrac{87}{2} \times 2.2 = 96$p per kg **M1 A1**

The price has gone up. **A1** **3 marks**

TIP

Remember, you are expected to know conversions like this.

4. (a) (i) $\pi \times 1.2 = 3.77$ m **M1 A1** **2 marks**

(ii) $\pi \times 0.6^2 = 1.13$ m^2 **M1 A1** **2 marks**

(b) your $3.77 \times$ your $1.13 = 4.26$ m^3 **M1 A1** **2 marks**

5. (a) (i) $24 \times \dfrac{120}{360} = 8$ **M1 A1** **2 marks**

(ii) $360 - (120 + 90 + 75) = 75°$ **M1**

$24 \times \dfrac{75}{360} = 5$ **A1** **2 marks**

(b) 'How did you come to school this morning?'

car	ⅢⅢ 1	
train	ⅢⅢ	
bus	ⅢⅢ	
walk	ⅢⅢ 111	

3 marks

You gain 1 mark for the types of transport, 1 mark for the space available for the tallies, 1 mark for the tallies being used correctly.

TIP

You did not have to include the survey question in your answer.

6. (a) 65 **B1** **1 mark**

(b) The differences double each time, so we need to add 32 to 33. **B1 + B1** **2 marks**

7. (a) (i) 33 cm   **B1**   **1 mark**

(ii) $\dfrac{4}{2}(5+15)=40\,\text{cm}^2$ **M1 A1**   **2 marks**

(b)

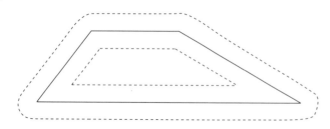

4 marks

If it is all correct you score 4 marks.

If not, you score 1 mark for drawing the straight lines outside the shape; 1 mark for the outside curved parts at the corners; 1 mark for the inside lines being drawn as straight lines, with no curves.

TIP

Remember in loci, a good technique is to keep putting in a few points that fit the idea until you can see the whole pattern.

8. Add the equations $16x=24$ **M1**

$x=1.5$ **A1**

Substitute $6+y=13$ **M1**

$y=7$ **A1**   **4 marks**

9. (a)   £1270   **B1**   **1 mark**

(b) (i)   £1000 × 1.06 = £1060   **M1 A1**   **2 marks**

(ii)   £1060 × 1.06 = £1123.60   **M1 A1**   **2 marks**

(iii) £1123.6 × 1.06 × 1.06 = £1262.48   **M1 A1 2 marks**

10. $4 \times 5 \times 12 = 240\ \text{cm}^3$ **M1**

$240\ \text{cm}^3 \times 0.57 = 136.8\ \text{g}$ **M1 A1**   **3 marks**

11. Use trial and improvement.

Trial (*n*)	Value		
5	3125	too low	**M1**
6	15625	too high	

hence $n=6$ **A1**   **2 marks**

12. (a)

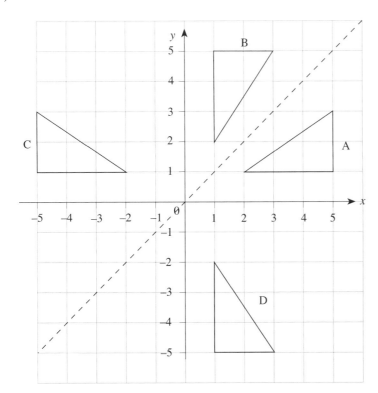

B1 **1 mark**

(b) $y = x$ **B1** **1 mark**

(c) (i) rotation, 90° anti-clockwise, about (0,0) **M1 A1 A1** **3 marks**

(ii) reflection in the y-axis **M1 A1** **2 marks**

TIP

You earn the method marks for simply stating the correct types of transformation.
Note that you need to state one transformation in each case. Do not be tempted into using
two different transformations to describe the change.

13. (a) $10x + 15 + 4x - 8 = 14$ **M1**

$14x = 7$ **M1**

$x = 0.5$ **A1** **3 marks**

(b) (i) $100 - 9x = x$ **B1** **1 mark**

(ii) $100 = 10x$ **M1**

$x = 10$ years old **A1** **2 marks**

14. (a) $D^2 = 8^2 + 11^2$ **M1**

$D = \sqrt{185} = 13.6$ km **M1 A1** **3 marks**

(b) $\sin x = \dfrac{11}{17}$ **M1**

$x = 40°$ **A1**

bearing $= 270 + 40 = 310°$ **A1** **3 marks**

(c) $BE^2 = 17^2 - 11^2$ **M1**

$BE = \sqrt{168} = 13$ km **M1**

Hope to Eden $= 13 + 8 = 21$ km **A1** **3 marks**

15. (a) $(10 \times 8) + (30 \times 29) + (50 \times 38) + (70 \times 17) + (90 \times 8) = 4760$ **M1**

$4760 \div 100 = 47.6$ **A1** **2 marks**

(b)

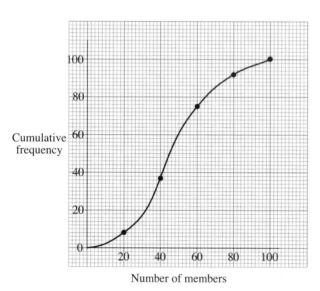

Number of members

2 marks

You score 1 mark for plotting the points correctly; 1 mark for a smooth curve or a polygon.

(c) (i) 46 **B1** **1 mark**

(ii) UQ = 60   LQ = 34 **M1**

IQR = 60 − 34 = 26 **M1 A1** **3 marks**

(iii) 65 members gives a cumulative frequency of 80 on the diagram. These 80 have below 65 members. **M1**

So only 20 churches can have ministers **A1** **2 marks**

TIP

If you know that you have problems with drawing a nice smooth curve, draw the polygon – it's easier.

---

16. (a) (i) needs a white ball $^6/_9$ or $^2/_3$ **M1 A1** **2 marks**

(ii) $1 - ^6/_9 = 1 - ^2/_3 = ^1/_3$ **M1 A1** **2 marks**

(b) (i)   Player 1   Player 2   Player 1

W   W   W

W   B   W

B   W   B

B   B   B   for all four **B1** **1 mark**

(ii) $\left(\frac{7}{11} \times \frac{6}{10} \times \frac{5}{9}\right) + \left(\frac{7}{11} \times \frac{4}{10} \times \frac{6}{9}\right) + \left(\frac{4}{11} \times \frac{7}{10} \times \frac{3}{9}\right) + \left(\frac{4}{11} \times \frac{3}{10} \times \frac{2}{9}\right)$ **M1**

$\frac{7}{33} + \frac{28}{165} + \frac{14}{165} + \frac{4}{165}$ **M1**

$= \frac{81}{165} (0.491)$ **A1   3 marks**

TIP
The 3 marks are a big hint to you that you will be involved in AND and OR, i.e. **multiply** then **add**.

17. (a) $1000 \div 1.7 \times 10^{-3} = 5.88 \times 10^5$ or   588 000 **M1   A1   2 marks**

(b) $1000 \div 2 \times 10^{10} = 5 \times 10^{-8}$ g

You earn 1 mark for dividing the correct way; 1 mark for an answer in standard form using the 5, and 1 mark for the '$\times 10^{-8}$' part of the answer. **2 marks**

18.

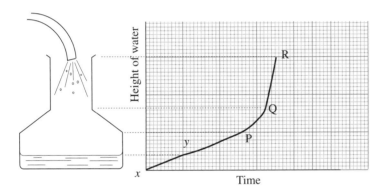

5 marks

You score 1 mark for the line xy continuing straight; 1 mark for this line stopping at height P; 1 mark for the curve to Q; 1 mark for the last straight line; and 1 mark for stopping at height R.

Total: 100 marks

How well did you do?

After checking your answers for each paper, compare your mark with the following guide.

- **A total of less than 30 Unclassified**
  You need to do a lot more work, learn some basic routines and try to understand more topics than at present.

- **A total of 30–44 Grade E**
  You have some foundation to build on. You do need to learn more basic routines and to practise the questions that regularly crop up.

- **A total of 45–59 Grade D**
  You are almost there, you just need more practice, then your confidence will grow because you will be getting well over half marks.

- **A total of 60–75 Grade C**
  Well done, you have reached the mark total that you need in order to be confident about getting a grade C. Don't rest here though, keep practising to maintain your momentum and that confidence.

- **A total of 76–100 Grade B**
  Excellent, all that practice and revision has paid off and you can face the exam with the confidence that you will be able to answer the vast majority of the questions correctly.

Longman – first stop for study guides!

We hope that you've enjoyed using this **Longman Practice Exam Papers** book. As a leading publisher of study aids for GCSE and A-level students, we have a comprehensive range of other titles designed to help you.

Studying for GCSEs

Longman GCSE Study Guides are designed to help you throughout your course, covering exactly what you need to know and revise for maximum success.

Longman Study Guides have already helped thousands of students make the grade –

"I found Longman Study Guides an absolute lifesaver"
"Longman Study Guides ... were an immense help to me and resulted in my achieving an A Grade!"

– now let them help you!

We have Guides for Biology, Business Studies, Chemistry, Design and Technology, Economics, English, English Literature, French, Geography, German, Higher Mathematics, Information Technology, Mathematics, Music, Physics, Psychology, Religious Studies, Science, Sociology, Spanish and World History. £9.99–£10.99 each.

Revising for GCSEs

Longman Exam Practice Kits concentrate on the subject's core topic areas, and provide students with everything they need to tackle their exams successfully and with confidence.

We have Kits for Biology, Business Studies, Chemistry, English, French, Geography, German, Higher Level Mathematics, Information Technology, Mathematics, Physics and Science. £4.99–£5.99 each.

Longman titles are available from all good bookshops. In case of difficulty, however, please telephone our Customer Information Centre on 01279 623928.

Good luck with your exams!

Moving on to A-levels?

We publish a comprehensive range of **Longman Study Guides** and **Longman Exam Practice Kits** for A and AS-level courses, too!

Studying for A-levels

Longman A-level Study Guides:

Available for: Accounting, Biology, Business Studies, Chemistry, Computer Science, Economics, English, French, Geography, German, Government and Politics, Law, Mathematics, Modern History, Physics, Psychology and Sociology. £9.99–£10.99 each.

Revising for A-levels

Longman Exam Practice Kits:

Available for: Biology, British and European Modern History, Business Studies, Chemistry, Economics, French, German, Geography, Mathematics, Physics, Psychology and Sociology. £6.99 each.

Understanding the Curriculum

Longman Students' Guides

Don't forget our **Longman A-level Survival Guide**, packed with invaluable advice. Also available, **Longman Students' Guide to Vocational Education**. £2.99 each.

Longman titles are available from all good bookshops. In case of difficulty, however, please telephone our Customer Information Centre on 01279 623928.

Good luck with your exams!